Growing in Discipleship

DESIGN FOR DISCIPLESHIP

DFD6

NAVPRESS®

BRINGING TRUTH TO LIFE

OUR GUARANTEE TO YOU

We believe so strongly in the message of our books that we are making this quality guarantee to you. If for any reason you are disappointed with the content of this book, return the title page to us with your name and address and we will refund to you the list price of the book. To help us serve you better, please briefly describe why you were disappointed. Mail your refund request to: NavPress, P.O. Box 35002, Colorado Springs, CO 80935.

The Navigators is an international Christian organization. Our mission is to advance the gospel of Jesus and His kingdom into the nations through spiritual generations of laborers living and discipling among the lost. We see a vital movement of the gospel, fueled by prevailing prayer, flowing freely through relational networks and out into the nations where workers for the kingdom are next door to everywhere.

NavPress is the publishing ministry of The Navigators. The mission of NavPress is to reach, disciple, and equip people to know Christ and make Him known by publishing life-related materials that are biblically rooted and culturally relevant. Our vision is to stimulate spiritual transformation through every product we publish.

ISBN 1-60006-009-9

Cover design by Arvid Wallen
Cover illustration by Michael Halbert
Interior design by The DesignWorks Group
Creative Team: Dan Rich, Kathy Mosier, Arvid Wallen, Pamela Poll, Pat Reinheimer, Bob Bubnis

Original DFD Author: Chuck Broughton
Revision Team: Dennis Stokes, Judy Gomoll, Christine Weddle, Ralph Ennis

Unless otherwise identified, all Scripture quotations in this publication are taken from the HOLY BIBLE: NEW INTERNATIONAL VERSION® (NIV®). Copyright © 1973, 1978, 1984 by International Bible Society. Used by permission of Zondervan Publishing House. All rights reserved. Additional versions used: THE MESSAGE (MSG). Copyright © 1993, 1994, 1995, 1996, 2000, 2001, 2002. Used by permission of NavPress Publishing Group; the Holy Bible, New Living Translation (NLT), Copyright © 1996. Used by permission of Tyndale House Publishers, Inc., Wheaton, Illinois 60189. All rights reserved.

Printed in the United States of America

3 4 5 6 / 10 09 08

DFD6 | CONTENTS

YOURS TO GIVE

Jesus told His disciples, "Freely you have received, freely give" (Matthew 10:8). We have the opportunity to pass on the blessings we receive from the Lord.

As the Lord transforms you, He opens new doors. God works through you to bless others. Sharing with others should be an overflow of spiritual transformation and is aided by personal Bible study. When you share, you will often find that it energizes your own life even more. God not only gives you gifts but also reveals new truths to you so others can benefit too. The Holy Spirit will frequently use your growth, words, and actions to significantly influence other followers of Jesus. Or your life may become an attractive fragrance to awaken an unbeliever to his need for Jesus Christ.

> How beautiful on the mountains
>   are the feet of the messenger bringing good news,
> Breaking the news that all's well,
>   proclaiming good times, announcing salvation,
>   telling Zion, "Your God reigns!" (Isaiah 52:7, MSG)

To help you grow further in discipleship, this study covers these topics:

- *What Is a Disciple?*
- *The Responsible Steward*
- *Helping Others Find Christ*
- *Establishing*
- *World Vision*

What Is a Disciple?

The simplest definition of a disciple is a "learner" or "follower." Socrates had disciples, John the Baptist had disciples, and Gandhi had disciples. But to be a disciple of Jesus Christ is unique; it involves much more than following any human leader. Jesus' followers were invited into a special relationship with amazing privileges and opportunities.

1. Read John 15:12-16. How did Jesus distinctively describe His role as master?

What were some privileges and opportunities for Jesus' disciples?

2. In Hebrews 13:5-6, God promises that this will be a special relationship. How do you feel about God's promise as you commit yourself to Him?

3. Read Luke 14:25-33.

   a. Why was this type of relationship not for everyone? (verses 26-27)

   b. What considerations does each potential disciple need to make?

c. Why do you think Jesus does not want any competing influences? (In order to more fully understand the use of the word *hate*, read Matthew 10:37.)

d. How do you respond to the intensity of Jesus' challenge?

" He is no fool who gives what he cannot keep to gain that which he cannot lose.

—Jim Elliot, *The Journals of Jim Elliot*

4. According to the following verses, what responses does Jesus say should distinguish the lives of His disciples? In addition to your answer, record a cross reference for each verse (many Bibles provide cross-references in footnotes).

Verses	Action	Cross-Reference
John 8:31-32		
John 13:34-35		
John 15:8-10		

5. Using the Scriptures from the previous questions, write a brief description of a disciple.

❝ So in the time of the disciples, someone who called you a follower of Christ would expect to see your life busy about relationship and reformation.

This identity was so clear in Christ's day that calling someone a follower would be no different from saying to someone, 'He's a trucker' or 'She's a doctor.' It defined the privilege and responsibility of their role as followers. It spoke volumes about who they were and explained why they lived, thought and acted as they did.

—Dr. Joseph Stowell, *Following Christ*

THE DISCIPLE IS A LEARNER

Jesus was a lifelong learner. In His early years we see Him in the temple, listening and asking questions (Luke 2:46). During His ministry we see him urging His disciples to "learn this lesson from the fig tree" (Matthew 24:32). The writer of Hebrews said of Christ's life on earth, "Although he was a son, he learned obedience from what he suffered" (Hebrews 5:8).

6. Solomon wrote many of the proverbs to those who would be learners. Why is it so important to remain teachable throughout your life? (Proverbs 4:11-13,20-26)

7. From whom can we learn?

Proverbs 4:1

Proverbs 27:17

Matthew 11:29

John 6:45

Hebrews 3:13

Hebrews 13:7

8. Why is it important for you to have a community who can provide guidance? (Proverbs 11:14; 15:22)

9. Read Proverbs 24:30-34. What can you learn about a willful, unteachable person who lacks judgment?

10. Do you enjoy learning? Imagine living the next decade without learning. How do you think that would affect your life?

THE COST OF DISCIPLESHIP

There is always a high cost for living. The key is in which price you pay and what the real rewards are.

11. What might it cost you to be Jesus' disciple? (Luke 9:57-62)

What could it cost you *not* to be Jesus' disciple?

12. Read Romans 12:1-2. How would you explain the meaning of the term *living sacrifice*?

13. Read Luke 9:23-26.

   a. What do you think it means to deny yourself?

   b. What does it mean to take up your cross daily?

   c. How can you reclaim your life?

> Discipleship . . . requires a basic shift of orientation as we align ourselves with God's will through humble renunciation of our own agenda. To deny ourselves in the context of cross-bearing means that the world may kill us for walking outside its path, but we are ready to do so, because God has called us to walk in a different way.
>
> —Darrell Bock, *NIV Application Commentary*

14. Prayerfully consider your life in light of the passages studied in questions 7–13. Are there ways you can better align your life with Jesus? What commitments might Christ be asking you to make?

> Cheap grace is grace without discipleship, grace without the cross, grace without Jesus Christ, living and incarnate. . . . Costly grace is the treasure hidden in the field; for the sake of it a man will gladly go and sell all that he has. It is costly because it costs a man his life, and it is grace because it gives a man the only true life.
>
> —Dietrich Bonhoeffer, *The Cost of Discipleship*

15. In the New Testament a life of following Jesus is compared to running a race. Read 1 Corinthians 9:24-27.

    a. How did Paul say we should run the race?

    b. List other important factors in running a race. How can these principles be applied to the lifelong race of a disciple?

    c. Is the way you are running the race of life today more like a fifty-yard dash or a marathon? Why?

16. Hebrews 12:1-2 gives additional insights into this race.

    a. What can hinder a believer from finishing the race?

b. How should you run?

c. Where should your eyes be fixed as you run?

d. In what ways does Jesus' life motivate you to run?

17. Read 2 Timothy 2:3-6, where Paul compared the believer to three types of people.

a. What are these three types of people?

b. Pick one of these types of people and further describe how such a lifestyle might represent a focused, diligent disciple of Jesus.

18. Read Hebrews 6:11-12. How do diligence and discipline relate to being Christ's disciple? (You may want to use a dictionary to help you understand the full meaning of these words.)

There are four steps in completing a course of action: desire, decision, determination, and discipline. For example, consider a person who desires to meet with God before going to work. He realizes that in order to have enough time he must get up early, so he decides to get up at 6:30 a.m.

The next day he oversleeps because his desire and his decision by themselves could not get him out of bed. He then determines to use an alarm clock to help him get up.

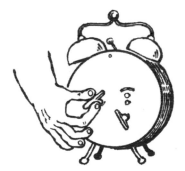

But the real test comes when the alarm goes off. Discipline must then come into focus. He must shut off the alarm clock and choose not to go back to bed.

Good habits can be developed as a result of consistent discipline. Consistency requires trust in the strength God gives. It involves heart, thought, and effort on a daily basis.

19. From Philippians 3:12-15, what attitude characterizes a mature follower of Jesus?

What attitudes do you think would characterize an immature believer?

20. What did Paul teach about diligence in Colossians 3:17?

21. What are some areas in which you
    should be exercising greater discipline?
    How can you do this?

22. In addition to discipline and diligence, what other heart atti-
    tude characterizes a disciple of Jesus? (2 Corinthians 11:2-3)

    What would it look like for you to be sincerely and purely devoted
    to Christ at this point in your life with Him?

23. Why is the attitude of your heart so important as Christ's disciple?
    (Proverbs 4:23)

Luke 9:23

Then he said to them all: "If anyone would come after me, he must deny himself and take up his cross daily and follow me."

Luke 9:23

Jesus calls you to be His follower, His disciple. Record some of your journey as a disciple. What has been most significant for you? What has been most difficult? Which of the characteristics of a disciple most challenge your life?

You may want to use this roadway to jot down key events, decisions, people, and God's provision in your discipleship journey.

BEFORE

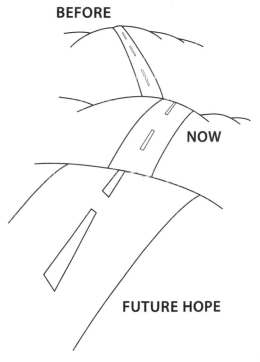

NOW

FUTURE HOPE

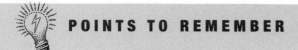
Review the chapter subtopics and use them as an outline to write your own summary of the chapter.

GOING DEEPER

Consider Jesus' challenge in John 12:24-25 to anyone who would be His disciple: "I tell you the truth, unless a kernel of wheat falls to the ground and dies, it remains only a single seed. But if it dies, it produces many seeds. The man who loves his life will lose it, while the man who hates his life in this world will keep it for eternal life." Compare this with Paul's challenge in Romans 12:1.

What would it look like for you to die to self (or to be a living sacrifice)?

If you consider yourself dead to sin and the world, how would that help you be a disciple of Jesus?

Finish this sentence with several phrases of your own: If I am dead to sin and the world, then . . .

The Responsible Steward

Stewardship involves managing what someone else owns. A steward is like the trustee of a fund or organization: Others trust him or her to wisely manage assets on their behalf. Because God bought us with the blood of His Son, all that we are and have—including our lives and possessions—belong to Him. As those who are accountable to God, we should become responsible stewards of our time, money, gifts, and bodies.

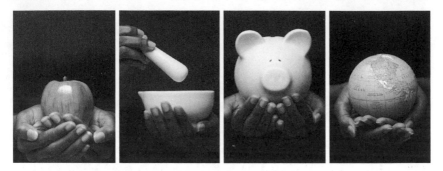

1. What did Paul say about the trust you are given?
   (1 Corinthians 4:1-2)

   Explain what this means to you. You may want to use a cross-
   reference to enhance your answer.

2. What are some areas in which you can be faithful with what
   God has given you?

   Proverbs 3:9-10

   1 Corinthians 6:19-20

   Ephesians 5:15-16

   1 Peter 4:10

3. What is the basis on which servants are found faithful? (Matthew 25:14-30)

> **❝** If the nature of God is to give, then we who share in God's life through Christ are also called to give. And what we are invited to give is not our surplus but our very selves in the service of God. Giving is self-giving. And this kind of giving is always costly. For in ourselves we embrace a small dying and a very real relinquishment.
>
> This kind of giving spells grace for the other and transformation for ourselves. As such, we will gain what in other ways we would never be able to gain.
>
> —Charles Ringma, *Wash the Feet of the World with Mother Teresa*

USE OF TIME

Every man, woman, and child has been entrusted with 168 hours each week. Are you investing your time wisely, or are you spending it foolishly? A good investment can produce a good return. How you use your time indicates what you really value.

4. Read Matthew 6:25-34.

    a. What two things are believers told to seek? (verse 33)

    b. What do you think is meant by the kingdom of God?

    c. Explain the righteousness of God.

    d. Now write verse 33 in your own words, using your descriptions for God's kingdom and His righteousness.

5. Read 1 Timothy 3:4-5,12. In God's value system, what comes before caring for the church?

6. Explain a biblical view of work from 2 Thessalonians 3:7-9.

7. Number the following items in order of priority as they currently exist in your life. Then number them again according to what you think are God's priorities for your life.

Existing Priorities		God's Priorities
	Job (your chosen profession or occupation)	
	God (developing your relationship with Him)	
	School (your educational development)	
	Family (your loving care and instruction of them)	
	Ministry (your personal outreach and witness)	
	Dating or marriage	
	Friends	
	Management of property and wealth	
	Serving the poor	
	Other (personal emphasis—social activities, hobbies, entertainment)	

8. After considering God's priorities, you may want to make changes in your weekly schedule so that what you do coincides with God's priorities for your life. Is there any change in your weekly schedule that you believe you should make?

You should continually pray over and assess how you invest your time so you can maintain the right balance in the various activities God wants you to be involved in.

9. Read Ephesians 5:15-21. What did Paul say about making the best use of time? How can you put his advice into practice?

Here are some considerations for how to make wise use of your time:

- *Prayerful planning—Listen to God. List things to be done in order of priority.*
- *Obedient selection—Respond to God's leading by doing the most important tasks first. In faith, commit unfinished ones to the Lord.*
- *Concentration and diligence—Do the task you select wholeheartedly.*

USE OF GIFTS

God has designed each person's appearance, voice pattern, abilities, strengths, weaknesses, and other characteristics, as well as his spiritual gifts. Each person is to participate in the body of Christ by demonstrating Christlike attitudes and by building others up through the use of his God-given resources.

10. The apostle Peter might have listed three of his strengths as enthusiasm, leadership, and speaking, while one of his weaknesses might have been impulsiveness. List three of your strengths and one of your weaknesses.

11. Read Romans 12:3-8.

   a. How should a believer view himself and his gifts? (verse 3)

   b. Summarize Paul's teaching on how believers should use the gifts God has given them.

12. How should we use the gifts God has given us? (1 Peter 4:10)

   Choose one of your strengths or spiritual gifts. How can you use it to serve others?

CARE OF THE BODY

Treat your body with care because it is the temple of the Holy Spirit. You will think and feel better when you have proper nourishment, sleep, and exercise.

13. Read 1 Corinthians 6:19-20. What does it mean for you to be a temple of the Holy Spirit?

14. Read Romans 12:1 and 2 Corinthians 7:1. What did Paul urge us to do with our bodies? Why?

15. What was John concerned about besides our spiritual well-being? (3 John 1:2)

16. From the following list, prayerfully choose an area in which you can improve the care of your body. What kinds of changes will you make?

Maintaining a proper diet

Exercising regularly

Getting sufficient rest

Avoiding harmful habits

USE OF MONEY

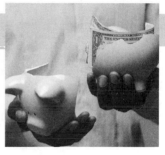

Jesus gave us a clear choice: We can either serve money, or we can serve God. To counter the temptation to serve money, Jesus called His followers to give money primarily as an act of worship to God and secondarily as a service to people. Our alternative is to give up worship of God in order to serve money. We cannot serve both God and money.

17. Consider Matthew 6:24. Why do you think serving money is in opposition to serving God?

    Whether a person has lots of money or very little, in what ways can he serve money? How can he stop serving money?

18. Why is it important to have the proper attitude toward money? (1 Timothy 6:10)

" Some of us have looked into the face of our idols and found that one of them is money.

Though we, along with millions of other church-goers, are saying that Jesus saves, we ask ourselves if we are not in practice acting as though it were money that saves. We say that money gives power, money corrupts, money talks. Like the ancients with their molten calf we have endowed money with our own psychic energy, giving it arms and legs, and have told ourselves that it can work for us. More than this we enshrine it in a secret place, give it a heart and a mind and the power to grant us peace and mercy.

—Elizabeth O'Connor, *Letters to Scattered Pilgrims*

19. The five verses that follow are related to the use of money. Match them to the correct descriptions.

a. Proverbs 20:10 _____ earning money in order to be generous with others

b. Proverbs 22:7 _____ warning about greed and finding our identity in our possessions

c. Luke 12:15 _____ danger of borrowing money and going into debt

d. Luke 16:11 _____ earning trust by the way we handle money

e. Ephesians 4:28 _____ warning about cheating others

20. Read 2 Corinthians 9. What principles of giving can you discover in each of the following verses?

Verse 6

Verse 7

Verse 8

Verse 12

Verse 13

Verse 15

a. Have you received a gift from someone who gave with a grudging attitude of obligation? How did that make you feel?

b. How do you think God feels when we give Him little or when we resent what we give Him?

Many believers find a regular plan for giving to be both scriptural and practical. Planning ensures against irregular or unwise giving or neglect. In a day when so many demands are made on your time and money, planned giving helps you honor the Lord with your possessions. Your plan may include these steps:

1. *Remember to whom you are giving. Your gift may benefit others, but it is primarily an act of worshipping God. Therefore, give with joy because you have received all from God.*
2. *Prayerfully decide what percentage of your income you will return to the Lord.*
3. *Set aside the Lord's portion first whenever you receive money. Put this aside to be used as He leads; once set aside, it should not be used for other purposes.*
4. *Prayerfully distribute the Lord's money as He directs. It is usually good to do this at a regular time—weekly or monthly.*

Make extra gifts and increase your giving as God increases your faith and as He prospers you. As you trust God with your material resources, He will trust you with His spiritual resources. He has committed Himself to this principle (Luke 16:9-12; Philippians 4:17).

The person who dedicates his money to God is dedicating himself—the fruit of his time, talent, and energy. The person who fails to dedicate his money has not fully committed himself to God.

Use the space that follows to record your plan for giving.

MY PLAN FOR GIVING	
Why I plan to give:	
My heart attitude in giving:	
To whom I plan to give:	
The amount I will give:	
When I plan to give:	

> Is "how much should I give" the wrong question? Have you ever asked God how much of your income — or time — you should *give* back to Him? Maybe we're asking the wrong question. Perhaps we should ask how much of all He gives us we should *keep* for ourselves!

21. Read Mark 12:41-44. What is the principle Jesus was trying to teach His disciples from the widow's example?

What is God saying to you personally from her example?

22. Meditate on Jesus' teaching from Matthew 6:19-21.

a. What are some of the dangers and risks that threaten our worldly possessions? (verse 19)

b. What are some things you regard as treasures in heaven? (verse 20)

c. When Jesus says, "Do not store up," do you think He is against responsible savings accounts, investments, or retirement plans? Explain. (verses 19-20)

d. Explain the truth of verse 21 in your own words.

Close your study time in prayer. Thank God for entrusting such riches to you. Talk with Him about how well you are managing whatever He has entrusted to your care—people, time, strengths, gifts, money, health, responsibilities, and so on. Express where you are in your desire to give top priority to His kingdom, His righteousness, and His treasures in heaven.

SUGGESTED VERSE FOR MEDITATION AND MEMORIZATION

Matthew 6:19-21

"Do not store up for yourselves treasures on earth, where moth and rust destroy, and where thieves break in and steal. But store up for yourselves treasures in heaven, where moth and rust do not destroy, and where thieves do not break in and steal. For where your treasure is, there your heart will be also."

Matthew 6:19-21

Journal about your journey toward being a generously giving person in a very materialistic world who is worshipping God and not money.

Review the chapter subtopics and use them as an outline to write your own summary of the chapter.

Do you feel as though you are a steward or an owner of your life, time, wealth, and body? What does it feel like to be a steward versus an owner?

What effect does your answer have on how you live this week?

CHAPTER

Helping Others Find Christ

God passionately desires to see all people embrace Christ and find salvation through Him. So He invites His children to partner with Him through their natural relationships. As insiders in our own culture and spheres of influence, we are strategically placed to introduce our friends and acquaintances to the Lover of their souls—through our deeds as well as our words.

"God didn't go to all the trouble of sending his Son merely to point an accusing finger, telling the world how bad it was. He came to help, to put the world right again." (John 3:17, MSG)

1. What is God's overarching
   purpose and plan for all people?
   (Ephesians 3:1-10)

2. What was God's purpose in sending Jesus?

   Mark 10:45

   Luke 19:10

   John 10:10-11

3. In Jesus' prayer just before He went to the cross, how did He
   describe the part His followers would play in working out God's
   purposes among those who don't know Christ yet? (John 17:15-23)

4. Why is it critically important to share Christ with others? (John 14:6; Acts 4:12)

5. When we share Christ with others, we are entering into God's ongoing work in their lives. How is the Holy Spirit actively engaged in preparing people's hearts to receive Christ?

John 3:5-8

John 16:7-11

1 Thessalonians 1:4-5

6. Read Matthew 4:19. What is the best preparation for sharing Christ with others? Explain.

As we partner with God, many of us face obstacles within our own hearts. Some of us associate almost entirely with believers because our fears and busyness keep us from forming quality relationships outside our religious circles. We may fear exposing our own struggles, sins, and weaknesses. Christ will help us overcome these obstacles as we follow Him into our needy world.

7. Read Matthew 9:10-13.

   a. What kinds of people did Jesus associate with?

   b. How did Jesus interact with them?

   c. List several people you know (friends, family members, classmates, neighbors, coworkers, social acquaintances) who have not yet met Christ.

If you have few unbelieving friends or family members, ask God to lead you into association with people with whom you can share Jesus and demonstrate His love.

8. Read the parable of the weeds, in which Jesus talks about living as members of His family in the midst of those who do not know Christ. Why do you think God wants us (the wheat) to continue to grow together with unbelievers (the weeds)? (Matthew 13:24-30,36-42)*

9. As you live for Christ among unbelievers, which of these fears (if any) do you have?

- *Being rejected*
- *Exposing your inadequacy in talking about the gospel*
- *Exposing your own feelings*
- *Exposing the flaws in yourself or your spiritual life*
- *Saying the wrong thing*
- *Being stereotyped and labeled as intolerant*
- *Losing friendship*
- *Failing*
- *Adding more stress to your busy life*
- *Negatively affecting your family by involving them with the unbelieving culture*
- *Being contaminated or losing holiness*
- *Living outside your comfort zone*
- *Fearing other believers' disapproval*
- *Other fears?* _____ **

---

* Adapted from Jim Petersen and Mike Shamy, *The Insider Workbook: Bringing the Kingdom of God Into Your Everyday World* (Colorado Springs, CO: NavPress, 2003), 18.
** Adapted from Petersen and Shamy, 32–33.

10. What encourages you from Paul's example of openness and vulnerability about his own struggles? (1 Corinthians 2:1-5; 2 Corinthians 4:7-9; 12:9-11)

LIVING AS AN INSIDER

11. What kind of lifestyle will reveal Christ and attract people to Him as God works out His purposes in and through us? (Philippians 2:13-16)

12. What practical guidelines for relating naturally to others do you see in these verses?

Matthew 5:13-16

Matthew 5:46-47

Luke 6:27-36

The simple act of greeting people by name can open up opportunities to develop deeper relationships with them. Learn the names of three people you would not ordinarily greet and write them here. Take the initiation to greet these people several times in the coming weeks. Write down what happens. Then look for small initiatives (a meal, an act of kindness, just listening) that you could take to strengthen these relationships.*

13. Early believers were recognized as followers of Christ by outsiders because of the quality of their love and their acts of service. Summarize in your own words the main point of 1 Corinthians 13:1-3.

14. Consider practical ways you could imitate Christ's servant heart by serving those around you. As you read over this list of biblical acts of service, write the names of any unbelievers you could serve in this way.

- *Give your time*

- *Offer hospitality*

---

* Adapted from Petersen and Shamy, 60.

- *Stop and listen, being fully present*

- *Weep and rejoice with people*

- *Show mercy instead of judgment*

- *Speak the truth in love*

- *Keep your word*

- *Hold your anger*

- *Apologize*

- *Be generous*

- *Treat an enemy with loving care*

- *Other? _____*

15. Not everyone responded positively to Jesus, so don't be surprised if some people do not respond well to your "fragrant" lives or words of truth. Why might some people resent or resist your attempts to share Christ? (2 Corinthians 2:14-17)

---

* Adapted from Petersen and Shamy, 62.

16. According to the following verses, what can you pray for those who have not yet met Christ?

John 6:44

John 16:8-9

1 Timothy 2:1-4

Jesus was sensitive to people's needs and spoke to the issue that was of deepest concern to those He met. The primary need of people without Christ is to receive Him as Savior and Lord. But people without Christ may feel they have many other needs that should be met before they consider Christ. You may have to meet "felt" needs before you can help people with their "real" needs. People usually want to know how much you care before they care how much you know.

CONVERSING THE GOSPEL

17. What guidelines are we given for talking naturally with others about our faith in Christ?

Colossians 4:5-6

2 Timothy 2:23-26

1 Peter 3:15

Here are some additional guidelines on how to have a spiritual conversation:

- *Talk about the realities of our shared humanity.*
- *Talk about the beauty and mystery of nature.*
- *Ask open-ended questions that deepen relationships.*
- *Listen closely to what the other person is saying.*
- *Reflect on what the other person says by expressing spiritual truths in non-religious language.* *

" Preach the gospel at all times. If necessary, use words.

—Attributed to Saint Francis of Assisi

18. Why and how should we use the Bible appropriately in sharing the gospel?

Isaiah 55:11

---

* Adapted from Petersen and Shamy, 72.

2 Timothy 3:15

Hebrews 4:12

19. Loving actions and service in the context of relationships can open the door for you to converse with others about your faith. Good open-ended questions can help you introduce spiritual matters into your conversations with unbelievers. Consider the examples in the chart that follows. Julia is a college student, David is a businessman, and Jason is a soldier. Following these examples, add the names of two friends with whom you would like to share Christ, along with loving actions and questions tailored to them.

Person	Question for Conversation	Loving Action
Julia	How have your ideas on spirituality changed since you came to school?	Help with laundry during test time.
David	What need in your own life do you hope to meet by having a successful business?	Offer to help with yard work.
Jason	Why do you suppose there is so much conflict and terrorism in the world today?	Go with him to visit his fellow soldiers in the hospital.

20. Name one unbelieving friend or family member you see regularly. Create some questions that would help you transition your conversation naturally into the good news of Christ. Also brainstorm practical ways in which you can demonstrate the love of God to this person.

PARTICIPATING IN A NEW BIRTH

21. From John 3:16-18, summarize the main points of the gospel.

Be ready to speak about Christ in any situation. Know the essentials of the gospel. Plan and practice how to explain Jesus Christ in a clear and interesting way. Then pray and take advantage of your opportunities.

After explaining the gospel, the key to helping a person open his heart to Christ is often a question such as, "Would you like to receive Jesus Christ as your Savior and Lord now?" If he would like to, ask him to pray and invite Jesus to come into his life as Savior and Lord.

22. In bringing a person to this point of decision, it is good to use an "action" verse to show him his part in responding to Christ's offer as the Holy Spirit prompts him. Choose one of the following verses and explain how you could use it in such a situation.

John 1:12

John 3:16

John 5:24

Revelation 3:20

23. What happens every time a person repents and trusts Christ? How does this make you feel? (Luke 15:7)

SUGGESTED VERSE FOR MEDITATION AND MEMORIZATION

1 Peter 3:15

But in your hearts set apart Christ as Lord. Always be prepared to give an answer to everyone who asks you to give the reason for the hope that you have. But do this with gentleness and respect.

1 Peter 3:15

What part did other people play in introducing you to Christ and helping you overcome your own obstacles to trust Him? As you journal about this, describe what most motivates you to share Christ personally with those you know who are still seeking Him.

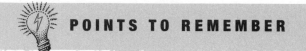

POINTS TO REMEMBER

Review the chapter subtopics and use them as an outline to write your own summary of the chapter.

Conviction of sin and the desire to receive Christ come from God alone. But He gives followers of Jesus the privilege of cooperating with Him in helping others come to faith in Jesus Christ.

People who have heard the gospel have reasons for not receiving Christ. You can become familiar with some of the more common objections and courteously point out how the Bible responds to them. This may help others see more clearly their need for Jesus Christ. The following verses apply to some of the most frequently given objections.

Objection	Verses
"If God is all-powerful and a God of love, why does He allow evil in the world? Why doesn't He stop it?"	Deuteronomy 30:19; Matthew 13:24-30; Romans 6:14
"I don't deserve the love of God."	Ephesians 2:3-5; 1 Peter 2:9-10
"Christians are intolerant people who have caused many wars."	John 13:34-35
"What about those who have never heard the gospel?"	Psalm 19:1; 97:6; Romans 1:19-20; Acts 14:17
"What about the errors in the Bible?"	Isaiah 55:8-9; 2 Timothy 3:16
"Why do so many educated people reject Jesus?"	Daniel 12.10; 1 Corinthians 2:14; 2 Peter 2:16-18
"What about all the hypocrites?"	Job 8:13; Matthew 7:1; Romans 14:12
"If a person is doing the best he can, God will accept him. Sincerity is what counts."	John 3:18,36; Romans 3:23; 6:23; Hebrews 2:3
"Surely there is more than one way."	John 11:25; 14:6

"There is too much to give up."	Psalm 116:12; Mark 8:36; Luke 18:29-30
"I will probably become a follower of Jesus some day."	Proverbs 27:1; Isaiah 55:6; Matthew 24:44; 2 Corinthians 6:2
"There are so many things in the Bible I can't understand" or "I must wait until I understand more."	Deuteronomy 29:29; Romans 11:33; 1 Corinthians 2:14; 13:12
"I'm really not such a bad person."	Genesis 6:5; 1 Kings 8:46; Proverbs 20:9; Isaiah 53:6; 64:6; Romans 3:23; Galatians 3:22; 1 John 1:8
"Maybe we'll get another chance after we die."	Luke 16:19-31; Hebrews 9:27
"I'm too sinful to be saved. God won't accept me."	Mark 2:17; John 3:17; Romans 5:8; 1 Timothy 1:15

CHAPTER

Establishing

What a privilege we have to help young believers become established in experiencing God's fullness! This encouragement of others toward spiritual transformation is a responsibility for all followers of Jesus. Some call it establishing or mentoring or discipling or follow-up after a new spiritual birth, but whatever term we use, it means partnering with God and others to help another become spiritually mature. While the whole community should be a part of this transformational process, we will focus here on one-to-one relationships. There is always someone who needs your help.

And I pray that Christ will be more and more at home in your hearts as you trust in him. May your roots go down deep into the soil of God's marvelous love. . . . May you experience the love of Christ, though it is so great you will never fully understand it. Then you will be filled with the fullness of life and power that comes from God. (Ephesians 3:17,19, NLT)

1. Read 1 Thessalonians 2:7-12.

   a. How did Paul describe how
   he sought to establish the
   Thessalonians in their relationship with Jesus? (verses 7-8)

   b. In what ways did Paul relate to them? (verses 7, 9,11)

   c. What did he model and do to help their spiritual progress?

   d. What was Paul's goal for his spiritual children? (verse 12)

e. In verses 8-11 Paul says that he not only loved the believers in Thessalonica but also demonstrated this love for them. If Paul had limited his influence to just instructing them, what impact do you think that would have had on them as they learned to follow Jesus? (See Helpful Tip in Going Deeper section.)

WHY ESTABLISHING?

Establishing is like spiritual pediatrics—giving continuous help to a young believer to stimulate healthy growth toward maturity and usefulness.

2. What did Peter compare spiritual growth to? (1 Peter 2:1-3)

a. Why do babies need help?

b. Do you consider yourself a baby in Christ or a more mature follower? Explain.

3. Jesus Christ wanted His love to be multiplied, so He gave His followers the Great Commission to reach the world with His gospel. What did He command them to do as part of that commission? (Matthew 28:18-20)

4. Why was Paul concerned about establishing those he had reached? (1 Thessalonians 3:5,13)

5. Read Colossians 1:28-29. Why do you think Paul was so intense and energetic about seeing people transformed in Christ?

THE WORTH OF
EACH INDIVIDUAL

God endowed every person He created with value and dignity. Humanity was made in the image and likeness of God. In the entire universe we alone have the distinct privilege of reflecting godliness.

6. Genesis 1:26-28 reveals our origin. Based on these verses, how valuable are people to God? From where does this worth come?

7. Read Psalm 8:3-8. How did the psalmist express the worth of people? Explain the significance of this for you personally and for others.

8. How many people did Paul mention by name in Romans 16? Why is this significant?

9. What does Jesus teach about the importance of the individual in Luke 15:3-7?

10. Read 1 Corinthians 4:15. Why do you think Paul felt personally responsible for the Corinthians? (Consider the difference between the heart of a guardian and the heart of a father.)

11. As you consider your worth and the worth of others, how does your heart connect with the truths of this section?

HELPING OTHERS GROW

12. What did Paul and his companions do to help those who had recently come to a belief in Jesus Christ?

Acts 14:21-22

Acts 18:11

13. What did Paul and his coworkers pray for new believers?

Colossians 1:9-12

Colossians 4:12

14. What could you encourage new believers to do? (Colossians 3:16)

15. In what other ways could you encourage and establish them?

Mark 5:19

Luke 9:23

John 15:10

Philippians 4:6

Hebrews 10:25

> The body of Christ needs us to grow through community and develop leaders who don't just manage but mobilize, empower, and release others into kingdom living.
>
> —Eric Sandras, PhD, *Buck-Naked Faith*

16. Paul used various methods to follow up with new believers. Which methods do the following verses describe?

    Acts 15:36

    1 Corinthians 4:14

    1 Corinthians 4:17

    2 Timothy 1:3

    How can you help someone you know by using one of these methods?

You will want to help a new believer in these areas:

- *Assurance of salvation and of God's love*
- *Regular quiet times alone worshipping God*
- *Scripture memory and meditation*
- *Bible study—understanding God's view of reality*
- *Prayer—personal conversation with God*
- *Fellowship with other believers*
- *Sharing Jesus Christ with others*
- *Growing in love, joy, peace, patience, and so on (the fruit of the Spirit)*
- *Learning to listen, trust, and obey God in daily life and decisions*
- *Serving the poor*

BEING AN EXAMPLE

" When it comes to follow-up, more is caught than taught.

—Dawson Trotman

17. What could Paul say about his example to the Philippian church? (Philippians 4:9)

18. Read 1 Timothy 4:12. In what areas should you be an example to others?

" Jesus' life provides the ultimate blueprint for whole-life discipleship. His disciples shared His everyday life—His highest and lowest moments. They saw Him from all sides, not just as a performer of miracles but also as a man who bore the Father's burdens, got angry, and even wept. His investment in their lives would reap tremendous returns after His departure. We, too, have deposits to make in the lives of our brothers and sisters in the faith.

—Pamela Toussaint, *Homemade Disciples*

19. Why is being real and authentic important as we touch the lives of others?

20. Can you say with Paul, "Follow my example, as I follow the example of Christ" (1 Corinthians 11:1)? What aspect of your life should be changed so that you can maintain a good example?

21. Think of someone you have had the privilege of leading to Christ or someone you know who is young in the faith. Remember to pray for him and consider what more you can do to stimulate his growth. Should you visit, call, or write to him? What practical resources might help him? Should you take him with you to see a nonbelieving friend or another young believer? Summarize how you can help him and what you intend to do.

Life-giving community breeds life-giving followers. . . . The early churches had a way of allowing the Holy Spirit to spend them on the horizontal, by serving and loving, while simultaneously having their own lives transformed on the vertical, through worship and study. That's the way of the Cross: to go and make disciples while we continue to apprentice ourselves to the Master Jesus.

—Eric Sandras, PhD, *Buck-Naked Faith*

SUGGESTED VERSE FOR MEDITATION AND MEMORIZATION

1 Thessalonians 2.8

We loved you so much that we were delighted to share with you not only the gospel of God but our lives as well, because you had become so dear to us.

1 Thessalonians 2:8

Reflect on how you were initially treated by other followers of Jesus as you began your walk with God. How were you cared for or neglected? In what ways did you feel supported or abandoned? What was most beneficial? What was least helpful? What can you learn about helping others follow Jesus from the way others have helped you?

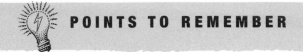

Review the chapter subtopics and use them as an outline to write your own summary of the chapter.

GOING DEEPER

Use Paul's first letter to the Thessalonians as a practical guide to help you establish a younger believer you know. As you read through each chapter of 1 Thessalonians, take notes on these questions:

- *What was Paul's attitude and heart (his motivation) for the people in Thessalonica?*

- *How did he relate to them and share his life with them?*

- *What did he pray for them?*

- *What did he do to establish them?*

- *What did he focus his teaching on?*

- *What did he not do among them?*

Helpful Tip:

One of the mistakes made frequently in person-to-person ministry is the assumption that young believers are ready for a structured and intense approach. But this approach can make them view Christian growth as burdensome rather than fulfilling. Remember that most people have never received spiritual help regularly in a person-to-person way. Rather than challenge, most of them need the encouragement of a "caring mother." Others who have a stronger foundation will be more eager for challenge and instruction as implied in the father-child relationship. Still others should be treated as mature brothers in the ministry.*

---

* Richard Cleveland, "Follow-Up: Person to Person," *Discipleship Journal,* November/December 1981, 11.

CHAPTER

World Vision

God is concerned for all mankind on an individual basis. With the billions of people in the world today, you might wonder how it is possible to have an effective part in communicating God's love to so many. We can do this by advancing the gospel so that spiritual generations will be planted and become fruitful all over the world.

" World vision is getting on your heart what is on God's heart—the world.

—Dawson Trotman

1. How do John 3:16 and 2 Peter 3:9 reveal the breadth of God's concern for mankind?

2. God reveals a wonderful glimpse of heaven in Revelation 7:9-10. Who is present with God, and how do you think they got there?

3. In order for the future envisioned in Revelation 7:9-10 to occur, God's plan through people must be fulfilled. Jesus invested deeply in a few people in order to see multiplication, and He explained what would become our role in God's plan. In what ways did Jesus state His Great Commission?

Matthew 28:19-20

Mark 16:15

Luke 24:47

John 17:18; 20:21

Acts 1:8

How does God want to use us to influence others spiritually?

It is certainly commendable to have the vision for reaching an individual, a campus, a military base, a workplace, a neighborhood, a community—even an entire nation—for Christ. But the Lord's concern is for the whole world, and this should be our concern as well. In the Great Commission Jesus gives believers the responsibility and privilege of reaching every person of every nation in every generation with the gospel. All our major decisions in life should be made with the whole world in mind.

THE WORLD TODAY

4. From the following passages, summarize how the Bible describes world conditions in the last days.

   1 Timothy 4:1-3

2 Timothy 3:1-5

2 Peter 3:3-5

Circle the conditions you listed that seem to be evident today.

5. What awaits those who reject the gospel of Jesus Christ? (2 Thessalonians 1:8-9; Revelation 20:12,15)

6. As Jesus saw the needs around Him, what did He ask His disciples to pray? (Matthew 9:36-38)

"Do you not say, 'Four months more and then the harvest'? I tell you, open your eyes and look at the fields! They are ripe for harvest." (John 4:35)

The total world population is approximately 6,499,358,843 and growing every second.*

"God was reconciling the world to himself in Christ." (2 Corinthians 5:19)

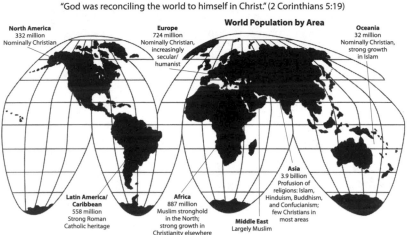

World Population by Area

North America
332 million
Nominally Christian

Europe
724 million
Nominally Christian,
increasingly
secular/
humanist

Oceania
32 million
Nominally Christian,
strong growth
in Islam

Asia
3.9 billion
Profusion of
religions: Islam,
Hinduism, Buddhism,
and Confucianism;
few Christians in
most areas

**Latin America/
Caribbean**
558 million
Strong Roman
Catholic heritage

Africa
887 million
Muslim stronghold
in the North;
strong growth in
Christianity elsewhere

Middle East
Largely Muslim

Source: Population Division of the Department of Economic and Social Affairs of the United States Secretariat,
World Population Prospects; The 2002 Revision and Urbanization Prospects; The 2001 Revision.

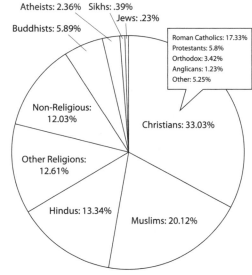

Atheists: 2.36% Sikhs: .39%

Jews: .23%

Buddhists: 5.89%

Roman Catholics: 17.33%
Protestants: 5.8%
Orthodox: 3.42%
Anglicans: 1.23%
Other: 5.25%

Non-Religious:
12.03%

Christians: 33.03%

Other Religions:
12.61%

Hindus: 13.34%

Muslims: 20.12%

Source: *The World Factbook*, "People," http://www.odci.gov/cia/publications/factbook/geos/xx.html#people
(accessed February 22, 2006).

---

* Data taken from the U.S. Census Bureau, International Programs Center, http://www.census. gov/main/www/popclock.html (accessed February 22, 2006).

"LOOK AT THE FIELDS"

Here are some practical ways to "look at the fields":

- *Use a world map to pray for countries around the world—that the people living there would come to trust Christ and grow in their walks with Him.*
- *Pray for persecuted believers and church leaders around the world.*
- *Correspond with missionaries. Learn about various mission fields and agencies.*
- *Read missionary biographies, books on missions, and missionary periodicals.*
- *Pray for your own daily contact with nonbelievers—that you will demonstrate the love of Jesus to them.*
- *Give financially to support believers and missionaries in another country.*

SPIRITUAL GENERATIONS

Keeping informed, praying, and giving are three important ways to help reach the world with the gospel of Jesus Christ. Even more directly, we can be involved through our personal focus and outreach. In all these things, we should continue to trust that God will multiply generations of Jesus followers around the world, whether we live to see this happen or not. This includes both spiritual and physical generations.

7. What was God's promise to Abraham? (Genesis 22:17-18)

8. Jesus lived in an agricultural context and thus used metaphors of farming and seeds and organic growth to illustrate spiritual generations. Read Matthew 13:31-32. How does God's kingdom grow?

Other passages you may want to study include Mark 4:1-20, Mark 4:26-29, and John 12:23-26.

During His last meal with His disciples, Jesus prayed specifically for them—both then and now. He asked God to continue ministering through His disciples to the lost people in the world. Jesus had planted seed for the future and was asking God to multiply it!

9. Read thoughtfully through Jesus' prayer in John 17:5-26. If you are a disciple of Jesus, then He was praying for you! Write down several observations about the following:

- *Jesus' vision that the world will be reached with God's love through generations of His disciples*

- *Jesus' prayer requests for us as we fulfill His vision*

- *How Jesus equips and prepares us to fulfill His vision*

Jesus loved the world and helped thousands, but He closely trained only twelve men. He saw spiritual generations multiplying through these disciples.

" Pursuing a divine vision is really an act of worship. It is a declaration of our confidence in God. It is a proclamation of how important we believe his agenda to be. And God is honored.

—Andy Stanley, *Visioneering*

10. As you reflect back over John 17:5-26, how do you see yourself in this prayer? What will you ask for regarding the ministry God wants to have through you?

11. Consider 2 Timothy 2:2. Have you asked God to give you one person with whom you can put this verse into action?

    a. You can help change the world for Jesus Christ by allowing God to reproduce His life through you in the life of another. Specifically, how will you allow God to use you in His plan for spiritual generations?

    b. If you have children, how will you trust Him to pass on your spiritual legacy through them?

    c. Are there other children you can minister to?

12. Are you investing your life, time, and money with the world in mind? What can you do to become more involved in reaching the world with the good news of Jesus Christ?

Remember to pray. Many of us cannot reach other nations on our feet, but we can reach them on our knees. And God hears!

13. Read 2 Timothy 3:16–4:8. Relate what Paul says here in regard to your life and to world vision.

SUGGESTED VERSE FOR MEDITATION AND MEMORIZATION

Matthew 28:19-20

"Therefore go and make disciples of all nations, baptizing them in the name of the Father and of the Son and of the Holy Spirit, and teaching them to obey everything I have commanded you. And surely I am with you always, to the very end of the age."

Matthew 28:19-20

How have you been impacted by Jesus' Great Commission to you? Do you accept this commission? Express how you hope to live it out.

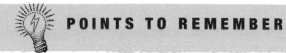
Review the chapter subtopics and use them as an outline to write your own summary of the chapter.

GOING DEEPER

To deepen your involvement in the Great Commission, consider these possible next steps:

- *Look through God's Word for His promises. Choose a few to pray over. Ask God to fulfill these promises. Imitate those who "through faith and patience inherit what God has promised" (Hebrews 6:12).*
- *Pray over John 17 and other outreach passages. As you pray ask God to give you significant ministry influence.*
- *Think about one or two individuals in whom you can invest God's riches. Have an attitude of expectation that in time, God will multiply that investment into the world.*
- *If you have children, intentionally disciple them. Pass on to them the spiritual heritage you have been given. If you do not have children, consider investing in others' children.*
- *Pray about, talk about, and hope for spiritual generations.*
- *Realize that salvation is personal but never isolated. It is for family and friends and the ministry context God gives. They all join God and us in His mission for the nations.*
- *Partner with others in Jesus' Great Commission. None of us can stand alone. Ask God to guide you to others who are committed followers of Jesus and then serve God together with them.*

Which of these would you like to focus on? How will you begin?

THE ESSENTIAL BIBLE STUDY SERIES FOR TWENTY-FIRST-CENTURY FOLLOWERS OF CHRIST.

DFD 1
Your Life in Christ   1-60006-004-8
This concise, easy-to-follow Bible study reveals what it means to accept God's love for you, keep Christ at the center of your life, and live in the power of the Spirit.

DFD 2
The Spirit-Filled Follower of Jesus   1-60006-005-6
Learn what it means to be filled by the Spirit so that obedience, Bible study, prayer, fellowship, and witnessing become natural, meaningful aspects of your life.

DFD 3
Walking with Christ   1-60006-006-4
Learn five vital aspects to living as a strong and mature disciple of Christ through this easy-to-understand Bible study.

DFD 4
The Character of a Follower of Jesus   1-60006-007-2
This insightful, easy-to-grasp Bible study helps you understand and put into action the internal qualities and values that should drive your life as a disciple of Christ.

DFD 5
Foundations for Faith   1-60006-008-0
This compelling Bible study will help you get a disciple's perspective on God, His Word, the Holy Spirit, spiritual warfare, and Christ's return.

DFD 7
Our Hope in Christ   1-60006-010-2
In this study of 1 Thessalonians, discover how to undertake a comprehensive analysis of a book of the Bible and gain effective Bible study principles that will last a lifetime.

DFD Leader's Guide   1-60006-011-0
The leader's guide provides all the insight and information needed to share the essential truths of discipleship with others, whether one-on-one or in small groups.

Visit your local Christian bookstore, call NavPress at 1-800-366-7788,
or log on to www.navpress.com to purchase.
To locate a Christian bookstore near you, call 1-800-991-7747.

NAVPRESS
BRINGING TRUTH TO LIFE
www.navpress.com